ethics

a graphic designer's field guide

Eileen MacAvery Kane

contents

Ars moriendi, ca. 1460, Engraving by Master E. S.

introduction

In *Thank You For Smoking* the main character, Nick Naylor, a spokesman for a tobacco company, states, "My job requires a certain... moral flexibility."[1] While every profession must deal with ethics in its particular field, graphic designers are trained to "make things look good." The very nature of their core mission inherently lends itself to a certain "moral flexibility."

Historically, graphic design has been an agent of moral and ethical thought. From the code of Hammurabi to illuminated manuscripts to the broadsheets used to spread the word of Martin Luther, graphic design has been used to visually communicate beliefs and ideas— to inform, inspire, and delight. During the Middle Ages campaigns like *Ars moriendi* were designed specifically to influence the behavior of individuals, in this case urging those on their deathbed from the bubonic plague to leave their money to the church. Soviet propaganda produced after the Russian revolution practically rewrote Soviet history. More recently the Obama branding campaign has been deemed one of the most successful branding campaigns for a political candidate.

When asked what the most important ethical issues are that graphic designers can expect to face in their careers, graphic design educators and practitioners have a lengthy list: piracy, spec work, plagiarism, copyright issues, social responsibility, cultural influence, intellectual property rights, image usage rights, crowdsourcing, legal contracts, sustainability, cronyism, and making boundaries were all mentioned.

By definition ethics means "the rules or standards governing the conduct or members of a profession," "a set of principles of right conduct," and "the study of the general nature of moral choices to be made by a person."

Using these definitions as a starting point, we can explore and discuss ethics in graphic design through three lenses:

1) legalities—the rules that govern the profession—copyright law, piracy, plagiarism, fair use, photo manipulation

2) integrity—principles of right conduct—spec work, crowdsourcing, responsibility to clients and contracts

3) morality—the general nature of moral choices to be made by a person—sustainability, social responsibility, cultural influence

Obviously these areas overlap. Photo manipulation involves moral choices as well as issues of integrity. Violating copyright law has clear legal consequences; however, it's also a matter of integrity. As the nature of ethics is not strictly black and white, it would be nearly impossible to look at ethics through a single lens without respect or careful consideration of its relationship to all areas of ethics.

This guide is designed to serve as a compass for the exploration of ethical issues in graphic design, provide resources for further investigation, and create an open dialogue among graphic designers about the critical issues of ethics in graphic design. It is not intended to be used as a sole reference but rather as a starting point for further discussion and reflection. Graphic designers are encouraged to use the resources included in this guide for more information and to seek legal counsel when needed.

1. LEGALITIES

overview

At first glance, the ethical issues that surround the legalities in graphic design would appear to be fairly black and white. With respect to legalities, "right conduct" is governed by law in most cases. However, further investigation reveals issues of debate.

For example, traditional copyright laws grant exclusive rights of ownership for 50 years and offers protection to copyright owners. Larry Lessig, copyright lawyer and Chair of Creative Commons, has challenged these laws. He contends that current copyright laws are antiquated and out of sync with contemporary culture. Lessig and other Creative Commons advocates feel that current copyright law actually creates a culture of lawbreakers and that alternative options for licensing images and other creative content will create a culture that is more likely to comply with the law and protect artists, instead of creating a complete disregard for copyright law and the consequences that ensue.

In addition to copyright law and fair use issues, font licensing, piracy, plagiarism, and image usage rights are some of the other legal issues that graphic designers need to be knowledgeable about.

copyright

THE COPYRIGHT ACT

Copyright is a form of protection provided by the laws of the United States (title 17, U.S. Code) to the authors of "original works of authorship" including literary, dramatic, musical, artistic, and certain other intellectual works. This protection is available to both published and unpublished works. Copyright defines who owns the work. Work must be original and creative to be copyrightable.[2]

HOW TO CLAIM IT

Until 1976, creative works were not protected by U.S. copyright law unless their authors took the trouble to publish a copyright notice along with them. With the Copyright Act of 1976, copyright is secured automatically when the work is created, and a work is "created" when it is fixed in a copy or phonorecord for the first time.

WHAT WORKS ARE PROTECTED

1) literary works

2) musical works, including any accompanying words

3) dramatic works, including any accompanying music

4) pantomimes and choreographic works

5) pictorial, graphic, and sculptural works

6) motion pictures and other audiovisual works

7) sound recordings

8) architectural works

These categories should be viewed broadly. For example, computer programs and most "compilations" may be registered as "literary works;" maps and architectural plans may be registered as "pictorial, graphic, and sculptural works."

LENGTH OF COPYRIGHT

A work that is created (fixed in tangible form for the first time) on or after January 1, 1978, is automatically protected from the moment of its creation and is ordinarily given a term enduring for the author's life, plus an additional 50 years after the author's death. For works made for hire and for anonymous and pseudonymous works (unless the author's identity is revealed in Copyright Office records), the duration of copyright is 75 years from publication or 100 years from creation, whichever is shorter.[3]

FAIR USE

One of the more important limitations is the doctrine of "fair use." The doctrine of fair use has developed through a substantial number of court decisions over the years. The various purposes for which the reproduction of a particular work may be considered fair could include criticism, comment, news reporting, teaching, scholarship, and research. The distinction between fair use and infringement may be unclear and not easily defined. There is no specific number of words, lines, or notes that may safely be taken without permission. Copyright protects the particular way an author has expressed himself. It does not extend to any ideas, systems, or factual information conveyed in the work. The safest course is always to get permission from the copyright owner before using copyrighted material.

CREATIVE COMMONS

Creative Commons is a non-profit corporation that offers ways to grant copyright permissions for creative work that make it easier for people to share or build upon the work of others. The Creative Commons licenses enable people to easily change their copyright terms from the default of "all rights reserved" to "some rights reserved." Creative Commons licenses are not an alternative to copyright. They work alongside copyright, offering a means to modify standard copyright terms. Creative Commons offers a spectrum of possibilities between full copyright and the public domain.[4]

CASE STUDY: "TOMOKO IS BATHED BY HER MOTHER"

One of the most powerful images of the twentieth century is W. Eugene Smith's photo "Tomoko Is Bathed by Her Mother." The image shows a child with a congenital disease caused by mercury pollution in Minamata, Japan. Although Tomoko's parents originally gave permission for Smith to take the photo in 1971, after Tomoko died in 1977 they were upset by the continued use of the photo and asked that the image not be used. In 1998 Smith's widow, holder of the copyright on the photo, complied with the parents' wishes and forbid future use of the image. This impacted exhibitions of the "One Hundred Greatest Photographs of the Twentieth Century" and also was seen as a disservice by those who felt Tomoko's image should be able to be used under "fair use" guidelines as it has helped in the fight against industrial pollution.[5]

PLEASE NOTE: Permission to use the image discussed in this case study, "Tomoko Is Bathed by Her Mother," was respectfully denied. The image can be seen online at masters-of-photography.com. The image below is from the same series and reproduced with permission from Aileen Smith.

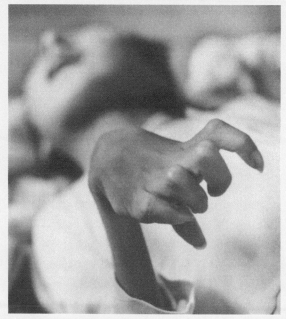

Image from "Minamata" Series, by Aileen Mioko Smith, co-authored with W. Eugene Smith

font licensing

Fonts are creative and intellectual property. Typefaces are the result of extensive research, study and experimentation, and for some designers the creation of typefaces is their livelihood.

The right to use fonts is licensed, and the right to use a font designed by someone else is acquired from the foundry that created the font and is granted in the form of an end-user license agreement (EULA). There are different types of EULAs depending on the use. There are standard, corporate, and site license agreements. Typekit is an organization that specifically offers font licensing for web use. Users need to check the agreement for the specific font they would like to license with the organization they are licensing it with.

If caught using a font without the proper license, the user will have to purchase the correct license for the font and in some cases pay damages to the originating foundry.

Using a font without the proper license also prevents the type designer from being fully compensated.

To ensure that you are complying with font licensing standards, you can use the following guidelines:

1) Make sure you have a license for all fonts that you are using.

2) When installing new fonts on your computer, make sure you also obtain the license to use it.

3) If you have questions about a font license contact the vendor.

4) Don't lend or give fonts to others to use unless you originally licensed the font for multiple users and you are sharing only with those designated as multiple users in the license agreement.

5) When downloading fonts that are available for free, be sure to check their license agreement for correct usage. The types of usage allowed can vary from personal use to educational use to commercial use.

" ...today's students seem to regard everything on the internet/web as "free" — it's there for them to take. Many of them don't realize that typefaces are designed by people who need to be paid for their work in order to pay their rent, and when they do learn this, many don't seem to care. **"**

—*Matt Ferranto*
PROFESSOR, GRAPHIC DESIGN,
WESTCHESTER COMMUNITY COLLEGE, VALHALLA, NY

piracy

Like fonts, software is also licensed. When you buy software you are purchasing a license to use it. It is the intellectual property of those who created it. Without permission from the manufacturer or publisher, it is illegal to use it.

In addition to being illegal and preventing software developers from being fairly compensated, pirated software can cause bugs, viruses, and system crashes. Users also lose the benefit of being able to upgrade and get support

Pirated software gets into the market and onto computers in numerous ways. People often don't even realize they are using it.

Following are the different types of software piracy that graphic designers need to be aware of.

END-USER PIRACY

- Using one licensed copy to install a program on multiple computers or servers
- Copying disks for installation and distribution
- Acquiring academic or other restricted software to use for an unqualified purpose
- Swapping disks inside or outside of the workplace

INTERNET PIRACY

- Online distributors offering special deals supposedly on behalf of the software publisher, such as inventory liquidation or bankruptcy sales

- Internet auction sites that offer counterfeit, out-of-channel, or otherwise pirated software
- Peer-to-peer networks that enable unauthorized transfer of copyrighted programs (if it's an upload of someone else's software, it's probably illegal)

HARD-DISK LOADING

This occurs when a business that sells new computers loads illegal copies of software onto the hard disk to make the purchase of machines more attractive.

To avoid this make sure you purchase your hardware from reputable service providers that provide you with a receipt of all original software licenses, disks, and documentation.

SOFTWARE COUNTERFEITING

This occurs when pirates deliberately and illegally duplicate and sell copyrighted material, often making it appear to their customers that they are purchasing an authentic product.

Illegally copied and sold software is not eligible for support, training, or upgrades. You may not be able to register it, so it may not work properly.

To ensure that software you purchase is not counterfeit, only buy from authorized sellers and make sure that you get the original user materials (manuals, registration cards, and licenses) and that you get a receipt with your purchase.

When working with outside vendors only work with reputable service providers that maintain licenses and documentation for the software that they use.

image usage rights

Whether you are buying or selling image usage, the rights to use photography, illustration, and other types of media varies and depends on a number of factors. Following is a brief explanation of the different types of image usage rights.

CONTRACTING FOR SERVICES DIRECTLY

When hiring photographers, illustrators, or other types of creative services (i.e. designers, song writers, videographers), a contract stating the terms of licensing should be agreed upon. This is in addition to a detailed description of the type of work that will be produced and the timeframe that it is to be produced in. It's important to understand that the rights to use the artwork are being contracted, not the copyright of the work itself. Like royalty free and rights managed imagery, the license usually applies only to the client contracting the services and for the specific project that the artwork is being created for.

If the client wants to use the artwork for additional projects, a usage fee will most likely be applied.

RIGHTS MANAGED

Licensing the rights to use content such as photographs, illustrations, or other media (i.e. audio, video) occurs when the seller of the license gives permission to the buyer to use the content in a specific way. Typically this includes restrictions on the length of time, the medium, the size, the format and the location of use.

ROYALTY FREE

Photos, illustrations, or types of media (i.e. audio, video) that are sold for a single standard fee and may be used repeatedly by the purchaser are considered royalty free. Usually the individual or organization that sells you the images still owns all rights to the images, and they are allowed for use only by the purchaser (i.e. the same images cannot be used by another company or individual without repurchase).

❝ I once had a client, a prominent museum located in New York City, who commissioned me to do a design for their yearly date book. Without asking they went on to use it for a number of other products. I called them and politely explained that they had only purchased the right to use it on the project they commissioned and that they would be charged a (small) fee for the other uses. They got all huffy and said that they would pay me, but that I wouldn't work for them again. Frankly, even though I love this museum, I didn't really want to work with them again either.**❞**

—*Eric Baker*
DESIGN DIRECTOR, THE O GROUP

CREATIVE COMMONS

Creative Commons provides free licenses and other tools to designate creative content for sharing, remixing, commercial use, or a combination of these.

Creative Commons licenses enable people to easily change their copyright terms from the default of "all rights reserved" to "some rights reserved."

Creativecommons.org is not a search engine but rather offers convenient access to search services provided by other independent organizations.

Some of the organizations offering Creative Commons licenses for images, audio, and other types of media are Google, Yahoo, Blip TV, and Flickr.[6]

plagiarism and appropriation

Plagiarism in graphic design means the unauthorized use or close imitation of existing artwork and the representation of it as one's own original work.

Appropriation refers to the direct taking over into a work of art of a real object or even an existing work of art. The practice can be traced back to the Cubist collages and constructions of Picasso and Georges Braque made from 1912 on, in which real objects such as newspapers were included to represent themselves. In the 1980s Sherrie Levine reproduced as her own work other works of art, including paintings by Claude Monet and Kasimir Malevich. Her aim was to create a new situation, and therefore a new meaning or set of meanings, for a familiar image. Appropriation art raises questions of originality, authenticity and authorship.[7]

In an article for *Design Observer* designer and author William Drenttel writes about how ideas come from many sources in graphic design: they recur, regenerate, take new forms, and mutate into alternative forms. In the world of design and photography, there seems to be an implicit understanding that any original work can and will evolve into the work of others, eventually working its way into our broader visual culture.

Drenttel goes on to talk about how the charge of plagiarism is not a simple one. He says, "Designers should take note: the idea of borrowing ideas is getting more complex everyday. Inherent in the modern definition of originality, though, is that ideas are extended, language expanded, and syntax redefined. Take a psychologist's ideas and experiences, as explained through the eyes of a journalist, and turn them into a play, a work of fiction—this is a work of complex, 'appropriation,' I believe the design world benefits greatly from such an understanding of complexity."[8]

" So much of what designers do involves working with other people's work. It's rarely obvious where to draw the line. Many people have a political point of view that more visual content should be in the public domain. I have been asked twice to serve as an 'expert witness' in intellectual property suits involving designers or artists. Both times I said no, because I have such mixed opinions on this question. Part of me does want culture to be free. But another part believes that artists do have to fight to protect their property.

When I was asked to be an expert witness in the Shepard Fairey case the call came from the lawyer representing the Associated Press. This was a case of artist-vs-artist and I could really see both sides of the story. On the one hand, shouldn't any picture of Obama be considered part of the culture, fair game? On the other hand, didn't the photographer work hard to get that particular shot? I said no. Too much moral ambiguity. Later, it came out that Fairey had lied about which picture he used. The morals become far less ambiguous, and Fairey ended up embarrassing the free culture side of the argument. Not cool."

—*Ellen Lupton*

CURATOR OF CONTEMPORARY DESIGN AT COOPER-HEWITT DESIGN MUSEUM IN NEW YORK CITY,
DIRECTOR OF THE GRAPHIC DESIGN PROGRAM AT MARYLAND INSTITUTE COLLEGE OF ART (MICA),
AUTHOR, CRITIC, LECTURER, AND AIGA GOLD MEDALIST

CASE STUDY: SHEPARD FAIREY'S "HOPE" POSTER

On left, Obama "Hope" poster designed by Shepard Fairey. On right, original AP photograph of Barack Obama taken by Manny Garcia in April 2006.

One of the most celebrated works of campaign art in American history, Shepard Fairey's "Hope" poster, was added to the collection of the National Portrait Gallery in Washington. The poster has also been the focus of a copyright-infringement lawsuit between Shepard Fairey and the Associated Press.

In early February 2009, the Associated Press determined that the photograph used in the poster is an AP photo and that its use required permission. At the time of the Associated Press' original allegations, Shepard Fairey's attorney stated that the use of the image is "fair use" and thus protected by copyright law. A few days later Fairey filed a suit against the Associated Press, asking a judge to find that his use of an AP photo in creating the poster did not violate copyright law.

In his February 9, 2009 Complaint for a declaratory judgment against the AP, Fairey claimed to have used an AP photograph of George Clooney sitting next to then-Senator Barack Obama as the source of the "Hope" posters. However, as the AP alleged in its March 11, 2009 response, Fairey had instead used a close-up photograph of then-Senator Obama from the same press event, which is an exact match for Fairey's posters. In its response, the AP also correctly surmised that Fairey had attempted to hide the true identity of the source photo in order to help his case by arguing that he had to make more changes to the source photo than he actually did and that he at least had to crop it.

In October 2009, Fairey admitted to the AP that he fabricated and attempted to destroy other evidence in an effort to bolster his fair use case and cover up his previous lies and omissions. In early 2010, it was disclosed in court that Fairey is under criminal investigation after he said he erred about which AP photo he used as a basis for "Hope." He acknowledged that he had submitted false images and deleted other images to conceal his actions.

As of April 2010, lawyers for artist Shepard Fairey were ordered to disclose the identities of anyone who deleted or destroyed records related to a copyright dispute over the Barack Obama "Hope" image.[9] Fairey's image has had an undeniable cultural impact. His red-white-and-blue poster of Obama with the word "Hope" at the bottom (pictured) has spurred an ongoing parade of parody images featuring everyone from Sarah Palin ("Nope") to Heath Ledger ("Joke").

Paste magazine's easy-to-use, web-based Obamicon generator—one of many online tools that make it easy to modify an picture to look like Fairey's poster—has reportedly created more than 500,000 of these images.[10]

At right, the author, Eileen MacAvery Kane, "Obamiconned."

questions for discussion:

1) Do you think current copyright laws protect artists or strangle their creativity and why?

2) What are the differences and similarities between traditional copyright laws and Creative Commons copyright guidelines?

3) Do you think the copyright holder owns exclusive rights to an image regardless of the feelings of image's subjects or their heirs?

4) Do you think "fair use" rights can be applied to any work that is being used for educational purposes or in support of a non-profit cause?

5) What are the tangible consequences of not properly licensing fonts?

6) What are the intangible consequences of not properly licensing fonts?

7) Describe the difference in how Typekit works compared to traditional licensing.

8) What are the different kinds of piracy?

9) What are the differences between rights managed and royalty free image usage rights?

10) Discuss what characteristics can be used to distinguish between plagiarism and appropriation.

resources:

BOOKS

Graphic Artists Guild, *Graphic Artists Guild Handbook: Pricing & Ethical Guidelines* (Graphic Artists Guild Handbook of Pricing and Ethical Guidelines, 10th Edition), Graphic Artists Guild, 2007. ISBN-13: 978-0932102133.

Larry Gross, John Stuart Katz,and Jay Ruby, editors. *Image Ethics in the Digital Age*, University of Minnesota Press, 2003. ISBN-13: 978-0-8166-3825-3.

ONLINE

ADOBE ANTI-PIRACY INITIATIVE
http://www.adobe.com/aboutadobe/antipiracy/types.html
Explanation of different types of piracy, implications, and steps you can take to avoid it.

AIGA: DESIGN BUSINESS AND ETHICS
http://www.aiga.org/content.cfm/design-business-and-ethics
Series outlining the critical ethical and professional issues encountered by designers and clients.

AMERICAN BAR ASSOCIATION
http://www.abanet.org/intelprop/comm106/106copy.html#copyrightis
American Bar Association Section of Intellectual Property with information about copyright.

CREATIVE COMMONS
http://creativecommons.org/
Resource for changing copyright terms from "all rights reserved" to "some rights reserved."

INTERNATIONAL TYPEFACE CORPORATION
http://www.itcfonts.com
Resource for creative professionals for buying and marketing typefaces.

TYPEKIT
http://typekit.com/about
Subscription-based service for linking to high-quality Open Type fonts for use on the web.

UNITED STATES COPYRIGHT OFFICE
http://www.copyright.gov/
The official site for administering and sustaining the national copyright system.

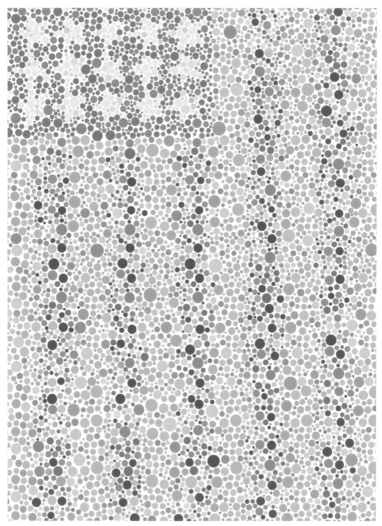

Designed for *Wired* Magazine by FB Design (The familiar shapes of the U.S. flag are reconstructed with colors and iconography from the flags of China and India and presented as a color-blind test to symbolize Globalization and a growing multi-cultural American population.)

2. INTEGRITY

overview

Synonyms for integrity include honesty and purity. When looking at issues of integrity in graphic design, the focus turns to how graphic designers conduct themselves professionally—the principles of right conduct that are understood and supported within the profession. Within the graphic design field, this quickly becomes a controversial topic. Crowdsourcing, working on speculation, corporate sponsorship, certification, and photo manipulation are some issues that graphic designers can expect to face during their careers.

In his book *The Power of Design: A Force for Transforming Everything*, author Richard Farson talks about when one thinks of a profession that one imagines that those who practice it would put humanitarian issues first. He states that we seek professionals' advice because we trust that their judgment is based on that special kind of wisdom that goes beyond the needs of business.[1] Like Farson, some feel that for designers to uphold their integrity they should move toward this level of professionalism and take a holistic approach that looks at systems with long term goals in mind rather than solving problems that are client-based with short term goals.

Graphic designers today compete and work in a global arena. Making decisions about spec work, altering images digitally, negotiating client contracts, and coming to terms about what their responsibility is to their clients and colleagues are just a some of the issues they face daily.

responsibility

❝ I think the biggest ethical issue will be from a
managerial perspective. Some bigger corporations
will try to use the recession as an excuse to place more
work on the shoulders of fewer people. Creatives in
managerial positions that work for these corporations
must balance the reasonable requests that some of
them make in response to the recession with the ones
that are borderline exploitative. The junior designers
in the field need to decide if they are being asked to be
part of an understandably lean and mean operation, or
if they are being taken advantage of. **❞**

— Florien Bach Leda
CREATIVE DIRECTOR, FB DESIGN, NEW YORK CITY
CREATIVE DIRECTOR, LATINA MAGAZINE

Graphic design is built upon relationships—relationships between the designer and the client as well as the designer and other members of the design team. Creative directors, illustrators, photographers, art directors, videographers, programmers, developers, copywriters, copy editors, project managers, and graphic designers are all collaborators in determining the success of a project. Not all projects require all roles and these roles often overlap or are filled by the same person, the designer. The most successful projects happen when there is a bond of trust between the client and the designer.

The most effective way to assure that the expectations of all the parties is met is to validate the relationship with a written agreement.

AIGA offers graphic designers a standard form of agreement in a modular form to allow them the flexibility to adapt it to different needs and different types of engagement.[12] The written agreement protects the designer, the client, and all vendor relationships. It describes the scope of the project, the timeframe for the project, and the estimated costs. It is the touchstone that all parties can use to keep a project on track—and on time. It should also state copyright terms and image usage rights—and address any issues of intellectual property. It's the responsibility of the graphic designer to make sure that the written agreement accurately reflects the scope and terms of the project.

AIGA has also written a guide for clients, "A Client's Guide To Design: How to Get the Most Out of the Process,"[13] which gives clients a detailed description about the design process along with expectations about cost and quality. It outlines what type of professional behavior a client can expect from a designer.

It also provides designers with a framework for the type of behavior they can expect from their clients as well as what type of behavior is expected of them among their peers and colleagues.

In addition to their clients and colleagues, in today's digitally connected world a graphic designer's responsibility extends to their responsibility to the world in which they live. Many graphic designers believe that they are responsible for the products they make with respect to sustainability as well as the cultural influence that they have. The organization "Designers Accord" believes that the creative community has a responsibility as a social and cultural force to create positive impact and support environmental social justice issues.[14]

work on speculation

Speculative work, or spec work—work done without compensation in the hope of being compensated for the client's speculation—takes a number of forms in communication design.

According to AIGA spec work includes the following:

- Speculative or "spec" work: work done for free, in hopes of getting paid for it

- Competitions: work done in the hopes of winning a prize—in whatever form that might take

- Volunteer work: work done as a favor or for the experience, without the expectation of being paid

- Internships: a form of volunteer work that involves educational gain

- Pro bono work: volunteer work done "for the public good"[15]

Proponents of spec work believe that it's a free trade system and actually gives young designers who don't have a big client list or portfolio filled with work a chance to be judged on merit alone. They feel it gives these designers a chance to gain experience, build their portfolio, expand their network of contacts, find more work, and if the work is chosen, be rewarded monetarily. Clients that are fans of spec work feel it gives them more variety along with lower costs.

Opponents of spec work assert that it devalues the design business. It also puts designers at risk of being taken advantage of as well as not being paid fairly or at all for their services. Graphic designers sell two things—ideas and time. Spec work, by definition, requires a designer to invest both ideas and time without a guarantee of compensation.[16] Clients risk compromised quality when research, the development of multiple options, and lack of testing fall by the wayside.

crowdsourcing

Crowdsourcing is any sort of outsourcing that involves a large group of people actively participating in the project. In graphic design it basically means that clients can send a project "out to bid." This means that they say how much they are going to pay for a design, and any number of designers can submit work for consideration. Clients can then decide after time and effort have been spent by one, or many, which design they like and are willing to pay for. The graphic designers whose work has not been chosen receive no compensation at all. In essence this gives clients the freedom to have multiple graphic designers spending time and energy on their project, and then they choose whichever design they like best and pay only for that one.

❝ AIGA, the professional association for design, believes that professional designers should be compensated fairly for the value of their work and should negotiate the ownership or use rights of their intellectual and creative property through an engagement with clients. AIGA acknowledges that speculative work occurs among clients and designers. Instead of working speculatively, AIGA strongly encourages designers to enter into projects with full engagement to continue to show the value of their creative endeavor. Designers and clients should be aware of all potential risks before entering into speculative work.❞

—AIGA's stand on spec work

photo manipulation

The images on the left from the Library of Congress show the composite image of Abraham Lincoln on the left and on the right the photo of John Calhoun used in the final composite for Lincoln's body.

In today's digitally connected world many people assume that photo manipulation is a byproduct of Adobe® Photoshop and they are surprised to learn that photo manipulation goes back as early as the 1860s. One of the earliest examples is Abraham Lincoln's head being placed on the body of the Southern politician John Calhoun.[17]

In 1994 the image of OJ Simpson that was used for a *Time* magazine cover was digitally altered to make Simpson "darker," more menacing.

Many feel that electronically altered images should be banned, or at the very least labeling should be required. The UK, France, and Switzerland are among those that support it.

Opponents claim that this would require banning, labeling, or warnings on a multitude of advertising materials. For example the roads used in car advertising are never as serene as they appear. If labeling is required for all digitally altered images, it would extend across a wide range of graphic imagery and require costly and time-consuming measures to enforce it.[18]

1994 *Time* magazine cover featuring OJ Simpson

CASE STUDY: MOVING PYRAMIDS

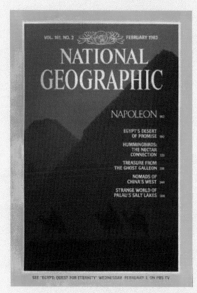

1982 *National Geographic* magazine cover

In 1982 *National Geographic* magazine published their February issue, and the front cover featured the Great Pyramid of Giza. Although there have been many cases of photo manipulation over the past several decades, this one was one of the first and the most famous.

National Geographic had a horizontal photo of the pyramids and wanted to make it fit a vertical format for the cover. They digitally altered the photo to bring the pyramids together. They referred to it as the "retroactive repositioning of the photographer" (which became one of the great euphemisms of our age), saying that if the photographer had been a little to one side or the other, this is what he would have gotten.[19]

Tom Kennedy, who became the director of photography at *National Geographic* after the cover was manipulated, stated that "We no longer use that technology to manipulate elements in a photo simply to achieve a more compelling graphic effect. We regarded that afterwards as a mistake, and we wouldn't repeat that mistake today."[20]

21

"FARM came at the perfect time for me when I was searching for something grounded to get involved in. I wanted to plant a tree or something- but this was better! I believe in what FARM is doing; a community claiming public space and growing food in a neglected urban landscape. This is an experiment that's allowing us to learn and play while creating a space that we can all enjoy and be empowered by."

—Ashley, CCA Architecture Undergrad

I am Robyn Weinton, a 29-year-old graduate student in design at California College of the Arts in San Francisco. I have a 6-year-old daughter. I am worried because young people seem unaware of the slow erosion of both environmental conditions and social services that has occurred over the last 30 years. I have never farmed in my life. I am a terrible gardener. (I will entertain thoughts of this now using these funny little dotted lines.)

Page from 56 page tabloid documenting F.A.R.M. (Future Action Reclamation Mob), an alternative form of non-violent protest, reclaiming public space to build community, providing services for underserved and transient populations and/or rehabilitating toxic land.[21]

corporate sponsorships

Used by educational institutions as an alternate stream of revenue, corporate sponsorships allow private industries to buy the naming rights for classes. Proponents claim that it allows them to keep classes running and that the corporations rarely get involved in defining curriculum. Critics contend that it compromises the integrity of the curriculum and ends up serving as an endorsement for products and services. In some cases the corporations also ask for the rights to the intellectual property produced by the students in the class.

" With the F.A.R.M. (Future Action Reclamation Mob) project, Kraft/Triscuit contacted me through a non-profit urban farm organization. They wanted to corporately sponsor the San Francisco F.A.R.M. so they could use it for advertising... to show their engagement in 'humanitarian' projects. In exchange for this, they would give us soil, seeds and a part time gardener. This would be the cheapest advertising opportunity money could buy—especially since we get dirt, seeds and a workforce via donations and volunteering. I'm not sure this caught me off guard, but it sure did get me fired up! I let them know exactly how I felt about a company that peddles diabetic-causing food to (mostly) children, wanting to associate themselves with an organic urban farm... as if they actually built it.**"**

— Robyn Waxman
PROFESSOR OF GRAPHIC COMMUNICATIONS AT SACRAMENTO CITY COLLEGE
AND COORDINATOR OF DESIGN EDUCATION, DESIGNERS ACCORD

cronyism

Cronyism is favoritism shown to friends and associates (by hiring them for positions or awarding contracts to them without regard for their qualifications).[22]

information is shared with only a select few and is based on "who you know" and not disclosed to all parties submitting proposals. Cronyism is an unfair practice and ultimately causes designers, vendors, and clients to suffer.

66 ...the ugly truth about design 'taboos'—work on speculation, plagiarism, piracy, work for hire, stock logos, cronyism, unsustainable design—is that they are being broken daily.**"**

— DK Holland
DESIGNER, CREATIVE DIRECTOR, TEACHER, STRATEGIST, AND WRITER

Cronyism compromises the quality of graphic design work and also prevents graphic designers from being hired for positions they are qualified for and prevents qualified vendors from receiving contracts. Cronyism also happens when information about budgets and competitor bids are shared. The process of submitting a proposal that includes budget information is standard practice in graphic design. Information about the client's budget and what the competitor bids are is information that is not meant to be shared. It's cronyism when this

kickbacks

AIGA's guidelines for designers states, "a professional designer shall not retain any kickbacks, hidden discounts, commission, allowances, or payment in kind from contractors or suppliers. Clients should be made aware of markups."[23] Designers are entitled to charge reasonable administration and handling charges. AIGA recommends that clients be told what these fees will be in advance. AIGA also frowns upon designers expecting payment for recommendations or referrals.[24]

professionalism and certification

Canada, Switzerland, and Norway are some of the countries that offer certification for graphic designers. Currently in the United States there is a movement to require certification for graphic designers. The topic is one that is hotly debated.

Opponents believe it's a waste of time and that design is a way of thinking that should be accessible to everyone. Others feel that certification would pose problems that would make it impossible to enforce. Still others feel it's about egos and elitism and won't add any value to the role of the graphic designer.

Proponents of certification feel that at the very least it establishes a minimum standard of professionalism and minimum level of performance regarding business procedures, education, skill, and ethical behavior.

Certification might also inspire designers to become more holistic in their practice and yield greater ethical responsibility across a wider field of practitioners.

Richard Farson, author of the book *The Power of Design: A Force for Transforming Everything,* states that people seek professionals' advice because they trust that their judgment is based on that special kind of wisdom that cannot be exercised in business.[25] Farson and his proponents believe that designers are driven by the needs of business and solve problems that are client-based with short term goals rather than taking a holistic approach that looks at the systems with long term goals in mind.[26]

Design certification models worldwide have different requirements. Common to them all is a council or organization that administers and upholds a set of professional certification standards for the industry as well as engages business and government on the design industry's behalf.[27]

questions for discussion:

1) Do you think it's unethical for a client to provide a designer with budget information that provides a competitive advantage?

2) Do you think designers are entitled to part of the profit or "finders fee" if they recommend a collaborative vendor to a client (i.e. printer)?

3) Do you think there's a conflict of interest if a job is awarded to a designer who is related to a client?

4) Describe the different types of spec work and what the pros and cons are for designers.

5) Do you think crowdsourcing is simply following a free market philosophy or undervaluing work? What are the effects it has had on the stock photo market?

6) Do you think certification would benefit graphic designers or put restrictions on them?

7) Do you think images and graphics should be labeled, i.e. "computer altered photo" or "composite photo"?

8) What's the difference between cronyism and a professional referral, how can you tell the difference and where do you draw the line?

resources:

BOOKS

Larry Gross, John Stuart Katz,and Jay Ruby, editors. *Image Ethics in the Digital Age*, University of Minnesota Press, 2003. ISBN-13: 978-0-8166-3825-3.

ONLINE
AIGA: DESIGN BUSINESS AND ETHICS
http://www.aiga.org/content.cfm/design-business-and-ethics
Series outlining the critical ethical and professional issues encountered by designers and clients.

AIGA: "POSITION ON SPEC WORK"
http://www.aiga.org/content.cfm/position-spec-work
AIGA's definitions of spec work, risks, and their position.

CANADIAN GRAPHIC DESIGN CERTIFICATION
http://www.gdc.net/join/index/articles99.php
Information about the benefits for nationally certified graphic designers in Canada.

FAST COMPANY
http://www.fastcompany.com/about
Articles about innovation that challenges convention and creates the future of business.

GRAPHIC DESIGN CERTIFICATION
http://designcertification.org/
Information about proposed certification programs in the United States.

NATIONAL PRESS PHOTOGRAPHERS ASSOCIATION
http://www.nppa.org/
Organization dedicated to the advancement of visual journalism and best practices.

NO!SPEC
http://www.no-spec.com/
An organization dedicated to uniting those who support the notion that spec work devalues the potential of design and ultimately does a disservice to the client.

1944 Nazi SS propaganda poster by Leet Storm

3. MORALITY

overview

Issues of morality are rarely black and white, and that is often what makes many people uncomfortable or anxious when dealing with ethics of morality in graphic design.

Some graphic designers believe ethics for graphic designers should be based on the idea of servant-hood and that helping other people is a good thing to do. The problem is that even if graphic designers were to agree on the idea of servant-hood, they would meet controversy when trying to define what "helping" is. The Nazis believed they were "helping" the people of Germany. History has shown us that their behavior proved to be quite the opposite. Others believe that visual rhetoric is a graphic designer's job. Like an attorney, it's graphic designers' responsibility to represent each client without being influenced by their own personal beliefs. They think that asking graphic designers not to persuade is like asking fishermen not to fish—it's what they are trained to do.

Issues of morality crop up in almost all areas of ethics in graphic design. Copyright infringement is a violation of law, but it can also be viewed as not being a "good" thing to do. Downloading fonts illegally poses a similar problem. However there are some issues that point directly to issues of morality and the role that graphic design plays in influencing culture. Graphic designers regularly create visual communication that's consumed by the masses. Issues like brand stretching, social responsibility, sustainabliity, and greenwashing all warrant examination through the lens of morality.

cultural influence

Graphic design serves as a filter through which much of our communication is disseminated. Graphic designers find themselves in the unique position of being gatekeepers of information as well as providing a mirror that reflects contemporary culture.

The influence that graphic designers have on how communication is delivered may not always be apparent to them. Often they are embroiled in the details of a project and don't even realize the impact their work has had or will have until some time has passed and the work is seen in retrospect.

Other times they are faced with a decision where the implications are apparent and they may be torn about whether or not they should create propaganda for a party whose politics they don't believe in. They also know that if they don't take the job and benefit financially from it, someone else will.

Advertising Age columnist Bob Garfield believes "political advertising is a stain on our democracy. It's the artful assembling of nominal facts into hideous, outrageous lies."[28] In 2004, U.S. presidential candidates spent over a billion dollars. In 2008 President Obama's advertising campaign was the third largest in the country, including an unprecedented online effort focused on positive messages.[29]

" A major ethical dilemma is to be hired to work for a client whose products, services or actions are harmful, criminal, politically unacceptable, or are promoting violence and war, or foster morally unacceptable opinions or actions.**"**

— *Steff Geissbuhler*
PARTNER, C&G PARTNERS, NEW YORK, NY

CASE STUDY: CASTING BALLOTS

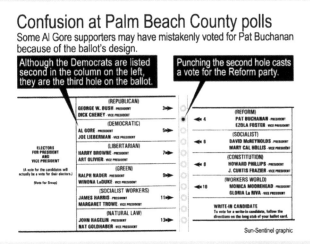

Confusion at Palm Beach County polls
Some Al Gore supporters may have mistakenly voted for Pat Buchanan because of the ballot's design.

Although the Democrats are listed second in the column on the left, they are the third hole on the ballot.

Punching the second hole casts a vote for the Reform party.

(REPUBLICAN)
GEORGE W. BUSH -PRESIDENT   3➡
DICK CHENEY -VICE PRESIDENT
                                                    ◄ 4   (REFORM)
                                                            PAT BUCHANAN -PRESIDENT
(DEMOCRATIC)   EZOLA FOSTER -VICE PRESIDENT
AL GORE -PRESIDENT   5➡
JOE LIEBERMAN -VICE PRESIDENT   (SOCIALIST)
                                                    ◄ 6   DAVID McREYNOLDS -PRESIDENT
(LIBERTARIAN)   MARY CAL HOLLIS -VICE PRESIDENT
HARRY BROWNE -PRESIDENT   7➡
ART OLIVIER -VICE PRESIDENT   (CONSTITUTION)
                                                    ◄ 8   HOWARD PHILLIPS -PRESIDENT
(GREEN)   J. CURTIS FRAZIER -VICE PRESIDENT
RALPH NADER -PRESIDENT   9➡
WINONA LaDUKE -VICE PRESIDENT   (WORKERS WORLD)
                                                    ◄ 10   MONICA MOOREHEAD -PRESIDENT
(SOCIALIST WORKERS)   GLORIA La RIVA -VICE PRESIDENT
JAMES HARRIS -PRESIDENT   11➡
MARGARET TROWE -VICE PRESIDENT   WRITE-IN CANDIDATE
                                                           To vote for a write-in candidate, follow the
(NATURAL LAW)   directions on the long stub of your ballot card.
JOHN HAGELIN -PRESIDENT   13➡
NAT GOLDHABER -VICE PRESIDENT

ELECTORS
FOR PRESIDENT
AND
VICE PRESIDENT

(A vote for the candidates will
actually be a vote for their electors.)

(Vote for Group)

Sun-Sentinel graphic

Palm Beach County Florida ballot from 2000 presidential election

The 2000 presidential election has been considered by some to have been decided by graphic design.[30] The layout of the ballot above shows the inconsistency with which the names were aligned with the holes that need to be punched. The problem is compounded because the line above "Democrats" points directly to the hole for Pat Buchanan. The line is longer and more prominent than the small arrow below it next to the "5." People of Palm Beach County were easily confused, especially those with poorer eyesight including the elderly. On top of this the hierarchy of circles was confusing. People tend to read in order. The list on the left has Bush, Gore, and Browne in the 1, 2, 3 spots. It is assumed that the holes would also be in that order and the second hole would be for Gore. The final factor confusing voters is that although we tend to read from left to right the black rules and column in the center breaks the flow from left to right and forces the viewer to read in column order, the left column first, then moving to the right. The results from the vote statistically were inconsistent with the demographic validating that the poor design confused voters and affected the election results.[31]

mass consumerism

In the 20th century graphic design became a valued tool for corporate America. This was exemplified when IBM legend Thomas Watson Jr. gave a lecture at the Wharton School of Business and coined the phrase "Good Design Means Good Business."

Opponents feel that our unbridled spending and greedy consumerism has led society to the state of recession where we find ourselves today.[32] The free market system is seen to be contradictory to issues of sustainability and encouraging social and community awareness.

66 The largest threat to humanity's future just may be the consumption of more than necessary. We are caught up in an unsustainable frenzy, spurred by rapid advances in the sophistication, psychology, speed, and reach of visual lies designed to convince us we 'need' more stuff than we really do."

— *David Berman*
AUTHOR, *DO GOOD DESIGN: HOW DESIGNERS CAN CHANGE THE WORLD*

Designers were generally seen as tools of capitalism. Creating brands, packaging, and marketing for consumer goods, graphic designers became an integral part of the free market system by contributing to the creation of wealth in society. Free market supporters believe that this creates peaceful relations and moral behavior.

All over the world consumption rates are soaring. At the same time millions of people consume barely enough to survive. Poverty is often blamed for environmental degradation. Poverty does tend to affect local environments; however, over-consumption is threatening the entire planet.[33]

CASE STUDY: IKEA— PLANNED OBSOLESCENCE

When browsing through all the products, space savers, unique designs that IKEA stores showcase, one eventually discovers that most of the furniture and products do not carry the signature

Consumers on their way to IKEA

of enduring craftsmanship. The majority of the furniture is a quick solution for people without a lot of space, time, or money, or in other words, for most of Western humanity. The unsubstantial wooden slabs and wobbly table tops are a marketing ploy—the furniture is not supposed to last—and consumers are comfortable with this. The argument that IKEA's popularity is due to answering consumers' needs is a short sighted one. IKEA is not an answer; it is a fix. When consumers buy an IKEA product they are buying a fashion product—fleeting, temporal, trendy. Trends change faster and faster as the 'need' for consumers to spend accelerates. The problem with mass produced consumer goods is not that they are cheap or even practical, but when critically evaluated as answers to what consumers want, they are little more than quick fixes for expected growing consumer needs. The unsubstantial products age and break and the need for replacements emerge.[34]

branding

Every branding expert will tell you that a brand is much more than a product or service—a brand is a promise. People fall in love with brands, trust them, develop strong loyalties to them, buy them, and believe in their superiority. Products are created in the factory. Brands are created in the mind.[35]

Logo for Obama 2008 presidential campaign

The 2008 Obama branding campaign has been deemed one of the most successful branding campaigns for a political candidate and cause. Branding expert Brian Collins asserts it's because they used a single-minded visual strategy to deliver their campaign's message with greater consistency and, as a result, greater collective impact.[36]

The design strategy focused on multiple platforms— cell phones, mobile devices, websites, e-mail, social networks, iPods, laptops, billboards, print ads and campaign events. Using shape, type, and color, the design team created a campaign successfully visualizing emotional messages that conveyed "hope" and "change we can believe in" across the nation and subsequently gained mindshare of the American people.

In his book *Iron Fists: Branding the 20th-Century Totalitarian State*, author Steven Heller asks, "how did a practice as vile as branding become so valued, indeed, the very mark of value?" Heller writes how in the past branding was used for slaves and criminals. Today, cities and colleges have joined toothpastes and soft drinks in the battle for "brand loyalty."[37]

Heller compares corporate-branding strategies—slogans, mascots, jingles and the rest— to those adopted by four of the most destructive 20th-century totalitarian regimes: Fascist Italy, Nazi Germany, the Soviet Union under Lenin and Stalin, and Mao's China. Heller asserts that design and marketing methods used to inculcate doctrine and guarantee consumption are fundamentally similar.[38]

brand stretching

Brand stretching occurs when companies use an established brand name to introduce unrelated products. The goal of brand stretching is to capitalize on brand recognition and consumers' trust. It can be a sound strategic choice for several key reasons: It helps to lower costs. It accelerates speed to market. It adds extra profits relatively fast while limiting financial risks, and ideally marketers expect that several products will promote each other under the same brand name.[39] It may also be used as a deceptive form of advertising. It happens when a tobacco company introduces non-tobacco products in order to circumvent advertising restrictions.[40]

"Joe Camel" and the stretching of the Camel cigarette brand is a prime example of brand stretching at its worst.

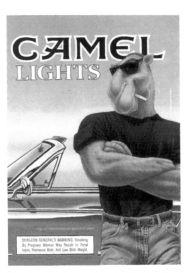

Magazine advertisement featuring "Joe Camel" and Camel cigarettes for R.J Reynolds Tobacco, 1993

Before the "Joe Camel" cartoon character appeared in the 1980s Camel cigarettes had one percent of the U.S. teen cigarette market. By the time the campaign was stopped in 1997 Camel had 32 percent of this market, and more than 90 percent of six-year-olds could recognize Joe (more than knew Mickey Mouse.)[41]

sustainability

Sustainable practices for graphic designers include a wide range of issues. When creating traditional print materials the toxicity of ink and paper and the sheer quantity of paper produced need to be considered. In addition to these factors there are other phases of the life cycle of products that need to be examined. To really determine the sustainability or carbon footprint of a product, one needs to follow it through its entire life cycle. Questions need to be raised about how much fuel is being used for shipping, what the final end product is, how long the life cycle is, and how long before the product ends up as waste.

In *Green Graphic Design* author Brian Dougherty asks graphic designers to start at the end of the process instead of the beginning. Imagine the best possible destiny for your design and visualize the process of every phase from the final destination of your product at the end of its life cycle back to the design studio. Consider everything from the time of its ultimate disposal to its conception including transportation, warehousing, production, and manufacturing that may prevent green solutions from being implemented.[42]

In *Cradle to Cradle: Remaking the Way We Make Things* authors William McDonough and Michael

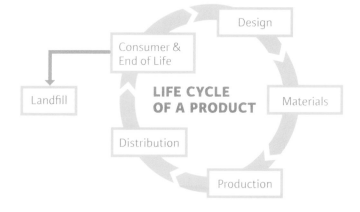

Braungart make a similar case for how sustainable practices need to be implemented. They assert that it's not enough for us to "reduce, reuse, and recycle." They explain how products need to be designed from the outset so that after their lives they will provide nourishment for something new.[43]

greenwashing

One of the biggest challenges that graphic designers face is educating their clients about sustainable practices. When companies claim to be eco-friendly based on a myopic view of sustainability and without looking at all the

" My biggest ethical issue concerns whether I am brave enough or care enough to follow that trail of manufacturing to learn that the product or service I am about to promote is the very thing that undermines me and what I care about. "

— *Robyn Waxman*
PROFESSOR OF GRAPHIC COMMUNICATIONS AND
COORDINATOR OF DESIGN EDUCATION, DESIGNERS ACCORD

McDonough and Braungart feel that when designers employ the intelligence of natural systems—the effectiveness of nutrient cycling, the abundance of the sun's energy—they can create products and systems that allow nature and commerce to fruitfully co-exist.[44] This important concept could also be implemented in graphic design practice.

implications of their actions, they may end up being guilty of greenwashing—the practice of "spinning" their products and policies as environmentally friendly, such as by presenting cost cuts as reductions in use of resources.[45] Sustainable practices need to be authentic. If they are not, they lose all credibility.

social responsibility

Designer Milton Glaser says that the ultimate challenge for designers is to create beautiful, not just sustainable, design. Glaser believes that we respond to beauty as a species; beauty is the means by which we move towards the attentiveness that protects our species as a survival mechanism. Glaser thinks that ultimately it's the responsibility of the graphic designer to inform and delight by creating beautiful designs.[46]

"Rosie the Riveter" painting by J. Howard Miller featured in the War Advertising Council's Women in War Jobs campaign created by the advertising agency J. Walter Thompson.

Social responsibility in graphic design has advocates in both the private sector and the public sector, in large organizations and small, and on an individual basis.

Since 1942 the Ad Council has been addressing critical social issues.[47] Campaigns like "Rosie the Riveter," "Smokey the Bear," and "Crash Test Dummies" have delivered critical messages to the American public.[48] A private, non-profit organization, the Ad Council uses volunteer talent from the advertising and communications industries, the facilities of the media, and the resources of the business and non-profit communities.[49]

Graphic designers like Tibor Kalman prodded fellow designers to take responsibility for their work as designer-citizens. Throughout his career he urged designers to question the effects of their work and refuse to accept any client's product at face value. Kalman inspired graphic designers to use their work to increase public awareness of a variety of social issues.[50]

"Portal 10" by Chaz Maviyane-Davies is from the "Portal of Truth" series and was a response to Robert Mugabe's announcement that European Union observers would not be allowed to monitor Zimbabwe's presidential elections.

The "Hurricane Poster Project" was conceived following Hurricane Katrina as a collective effort by the design community to unite and effect change through their work. The project sold limited edition sets of hurricane-related posters from high-profile and up-and-coming artists, designers, and firms from the United States and abroad. The donated posters were sold online, and all profits went directly to the Red Cross.[51]

Organizations like "Design Ignites Change" engage high school and college students in design and architecture projects that address pressing social issues. Participants are encouraged to apply design thinking to problems that exist in their own communities.[52]

Across the globe as well as on an individual level, graphic designers are being challenged to create work that's socially responsible.

❝ Being a part of a project as big and rewarding as 'Water for India' allowed me to realize first-hand that design is not just about marketing a product or making a bottom line, but rather it can be rewarding on a human scale. Working with 'Engineers Without Borders' showed me design can be collaborative and used for the greater good. I want to continue these projects after I graduate. ❞

— *Alexander Sangeorge*

HARTFORD ART SCHOOL ALUMNI AND TEAM MEMBER OF "WATER FOR INDIA"

CASE STUDY: "WATER FOR INDIA"

Design team in front of the mural with the children and villagers. Left to right: Tomasz Kazmierczak (light red shirt), Constanza Gowen Segovia (blue shirt), Ashley Gummelt (white shirt), Alexander Sangeorge (plaid shirt), Parker Hu (grey shirt, with scarf), Professor Natacha Poggio (orange shirt). Other team members not shown include Jackie Minkler and Kim Herrmannsdoerfer.

In January 2009, Hartford Art School Professor Natacha Poggio and a team of six art and design students traveled to Abheypur, India to implement the "Water for India" sanitation campaign as partners to the work of the "Engineers Without Borders" Student Chapter at the University of Hartford.

"Water for India" aims to convey the importance of cleanliness, sharing, and respect for water resources. During the January trip, the team painted a mural at the girls' primary school and distributed coloring books with sanitation tips as well as t-shirts with the campaign logo.

What began as an assignment in the Spring of 2008 for a class called "Issues in Design" grew into an ongoing effort after receiving feedback from Abheypur's villagers. Since the start of the project, the students worked collaboratively on this wide-reaching project with other disciplines, team members and cultures. The students and Professor Poggio have continued using design as a way to educate and empower

Constanza Gowen Segovia working on detail of mural.

people. The social consciousness and awareness of those involved grew through the process of research and learning to design for a more universal audience.

The mission was extended in the next session of "Issues in Design" where the students worked on a new wellness campaign designing "kangas" (traditional cotton garments that Sub-Saharan women wear) for local communities in the Lake Victoria region of Kenya.

Professor Poggio continues to teach "Issues in Design" along with a special topics class called "Design Global Change" (DGC), which focuses on global design projects.[53]

Left and center, final campaign banners. Right, early version of a banner. The design team drew inspiration from Indian rangoli (sand painting decorations). ©Design Global Change.

questions for discussion:

1) Do you think a designer is responsible for how content is perceived? Discuss at least 3 ways that a designer can affect the way content is received.

2) What similarities do you see between the Obama branding and Nazi branding campaigns? What differences do you see?

3) In what ways can designers implement green practices and also educate their clients?

4) Do you think designers have a responsibility to do pro bono work?

5) Do you think designers have a responsibility to represent their clients and their products, regardless of their personal views?

6) Discuss how cradle-to-cradle design can be profitable.

7) Do you think a graphic designer should promote his or her own values?

8) Do you think graphic designers have a responsibility to use their skills to promote issues of sustainability and social awareness?

9) Do you think doing pro-bono work is the same as working on speculation and devalues the work that graphic designers do?

resources:

BOOKS

David B. Berman. *Do Good Design: How Designers Can Change The World*. Berkeley, CA: New Riders. ISBN 13:978-0-321-57320-9.

Brian Dougherty, *Green Graphic Design*. New York, NY: Allworth Press, 2008. ISBN 13:978-1-58115-511-2

William McDonough and Michael Braungart. *Cradle To Cradle: Remaking the Way We Make Things*. New York, NY: North Point Press, 2002. ISBN 13:978-0-86547-587-8

Lucienne Roberts. *Good: Ethics of Graphic Design*. Lausanne, Switzerland: AVA Publishing SA., 2006.ISBN 2-940373-14-0.

ONLINE

AD COUNCIL
http://www.adcouncil.org/
Organization that uses voluntary resources to create Public Service Ads (PSAs).

DESIGNERS ACCORD
http://www.designersaccord.org/
A collective organization of designers, educators, and business leaders devoted to innovative and sustainable problem solving throughout the creative community.

DESIGN GLOBAL CHANGE
http://designglobalchange.org/
A creative think-tank, applying the power of design to develop projects that bring positive change to communities around the world.

DESIGN IGNITES CHANGE
http://designigniteschange.org/
Collaboration between the Adobe Foundation and Worldstudio, engaging high school and college students in multidisciplinary design and architecture projects that address pressing social issues.

LEARN AND SERVE AMERICA
http://www.learnandserve.gov/
Learn and Serve America supports and encourages service-learning throughout the United States.

THE LIVING PRINCIPLES
http://www.livingprinciples.org/
A guide for those who use design thinking to create positive cultural change.

LOVELY AS A TREE
http://lovelyasatree.com/
Information about how graphic design materials impact the environment.

RENOURISH
http://re-nourish.com/?l=home
Tools and resources to build a more sustainable practice.

notes

INTRODUCTION

1 http://www.imdb.com/title/tt0427944/quotes.

LEGALITIES

2 http://www.copyright.gov/circs/circ1.pdf.

3 http://www.copyright.gov/fls/fl102.html.

4 http://creativecommons.org/about/.

5 http://www.masters-of-photography.com/S/smith/smith_minamata_full.html

6 http://creativecommons.org/about/.

7 http://www.tate.org.uk/collections/glossary/definition.jsp?entryId=23.

8 http://www.designobserver.com/observatory/entry.html?entry=2837.

9 http://www.wired.com/underwire/2009/02/copyfight-erupt/.

10 http://www.ap.org/iprights/fairey.html.

INTEGRITY

11 Richard Farson, *The Power of Design: A Force for Transforming*, 2008.

12 AIGA, *Standard Form of Agreement for Design Services*, 2009.

13 AIGA, *A Client's Guide To Design: How to Get the Most Out of the Process*, 2009.

14 http://www.designersaccord.org/faq/.

15 http://www.aiga.org/content.cfm/position-spec-work#spec-types.

16 http://www.no-spec.com/articles/ten-reasons/.

17 http://www.cs.dartmouth.edu/farid/research/digitaltampering/.

18 http://ethicist.blogs.nytimes.com/2009/10/20/should-photos-come-with-warning-labels/.

19 http://www.nppa.org/professional_development/self-training_resources/eadp_report/digital_manipulation.html.

20 http://www.cs.dartmouth.edu/farid/research/digitaltampering/.

21 http://www.thinkdiscussact.org/farm/.

22 http://wordnetweb.princeton.edu/perl/webwn?s=cronyism.

23 AIGA, *Design Business + Ethics*, 2009.

24 AIGA, *Design Business + Ethics*, 2009.

25 Richard Farson, *The Power of Design: A Force for Transforming*, 2008.

26 Richard Farson, *The Power of Design: A Force for Transforming*, 2008.

MORALITY

27 http://designcertification.org/.

28 http://www.will-harris.com/wire/html/design_ramifications.html.

29 David B. Berman, *Do Good Design: How Designers Can Change The World*, 2009.

30 http://www.will-harris.com/wire/html/design_ramifications.html.

31 http://www.will-harris.com/wire/html/design_ramifications.html.

32 http://www.pbs.org/wgbh/pages/frontline/warning/themes/greenspan.html.

33 http://www.storyofstuff.com/.

34 http://social-activism.suite101.com/article.cfm/ikea_and_consumption.

35 Alina Wheeler, *Designing Brand Identity*, 2006.

36 http://campaignstops.blogs.nytimes.com/2008/04/02/to-the-letter-born/.

37 http://www.nytimes.com/2008/07/31/arts/31iht-IDLEDE2.1.14885119.html?_r=1.

38 http://www.nytimes.com/2008/07/31/arts/31iht-IDLEDE2.1.14885119.html?_r=1.

39 http://www.yourdictionary.com/business/brand-stretching.

40 http://www.allbusiness.com/management/1045288-1.html.

41 David B. Berman, *Do Good Design: How Designers Can Change The World*, 2009.

42 Brian Dougherty, *Green Graphic Design*, 2009.

43 http://www.mcdonough.com/cradle_to_cradle.htm.

44 http://www.mcdonough.com/cradle_to_cradle.htm.

45 http://www.businessethics.ca/greenwashing/.

46 http://bigthink.com/miltonglaser/big-think-interview-with-milton-glaser.

47 http://www.adcouncil.org/.

48 http://www.adcouncil.org/timeline.html.

49 http://www.adcouncil.org/.

50 http://www.aiga.org/content.cfm/medalist-tiborkalman.

51 http://www.thehurricaneposterproject.com/index.php?page=poster.

52 http://designigniteschange.org/pages/2-about.

53 http://designglobalchange.org/.

image credits

iv   *Ars moriendi*. (Source: http://www.payer.de/buddhpsych/psycho557.jpg)

4   Image 014 from *Minamata* series, by Aileen Mioko Smith, co-authored with W. Eugene Smith. Reprinted by permission of Aileen Mioko Smith.

12   Obama "HOPE" poster. (Source: http://www.flickr.com/photos/ocean_of_stars/3254892746/)

13   "Obamiconned." (Source: http://obamiconme.pastemagazine.com/entries/new_obamicon.html)

18   *Wired* Magazine illustration by FB Design. Reprinted courtesy of Florien Bach Leda.

22   "Abraham Lincoln/John Calhoun." (Source: http://www.cs.dartmouth.edu/farid/research/digitaltampering/)

22   *Time* magazine cover. (Source: http://www.cs.dartmouth.edu/farid/research/digitaltampering/)

23   *National Geographic* magazine cover. (Source: http://www.cs.dartmouth.edu/farid/research/digitaltampering/)

24   "Ashley," p. 56 tabloid documenting F.A.R.M. Reprinted courtesy of Robyn Waxman.

30   "Nazi SS Propaganda" poster. (Source: http://www.flickr.com/photos/pixel-jones/4449101481/)

33   "Palm Beach County Florida ballot." (Source: http://www.will-harris.com/wire/html/design_ramifications.html)

35   "IKEA Store." (Source: http://www.flickr.com/photos/claytanic/2924792908/sizes/l/)

37   "Joe Camel." (Source: http://www.bambootrading.com/proddetail.asp?prod=1385, p. 39

40   "Rosie the Riveter" poster. (Source: http://www.flickr.com/photos/modestchanges/3214701196/sizes/o/)

41   "Water for India" group photo. Reprinted courtesy of Natacha Poggio, ©Design Global Change.

42   "Constanza Gowen Segovia." Reprinted courtesy of Natacha Poggio, ©Design Global Change.

42   "Water for India" campaign banners. Reprinted courtesy of Natacha Poggio, ©Design Global Change.

acknowledgments

A special thanks goes to Professor Trudy Abadie of Savannah College of Art and Design for her never-ending support from the conception of this project to its fruition. I also owe many thanks to my editor, Jennifer Peper, for her invaluable feedback and support.

I would also like to thank the many graphic design educators, practitioners, and students who contributed to this project with their heartfelt and candid feedback.

Last, but not least, my gratitude to my husband Rob and son Joe for their everlasting love and support.

index

COLOPHON

BOOK DESIGN: Eileen MacAvery Kane

EDITOR: Jennifer Peper

TYPOGRAPHY: Karmina Serif and Karmina Sans Serif designed by Veronika Burian
and José Scaglione of Type Together, 2007.

ABOUT THE AUTHOR

Eileen MacAvery Kane has over twenty-five years of experience as an art director and
graphic designer working for IBM, International Paper, ABC Television, Home Box Office,
Hallmark Channel, Smithsonian Magazine, Bethel Woods Center for the Arts, and Omega
Institute. The creation of this handbook was done in part for the completion of her MFA in
Graphic Design from Savannah College of Art and Design. A Hudson Valley native, Eileen
teaches classes in digital art and design, is a member of Artists in the Parks, and serves on
the board of Safe Harbors of the Hudson, an organization dedicated to transforming lives
and building communities through housing and the arts. eileenmacaverykane.com

CPSIA information can be obtained
at www.ICGtesting.com
Printed in the USA
LVIW011541151012

302950LV00001B